ABUNDANT TRUTH INTERNATIONAL MINISTRIES

Abundant Truth Leadership Series

Motives In Ministry

Defining the Proper Motives for Ministry and Service

Roderick Levi Evans

Motives In Ministry
Defining the Proper Motives for Ministry and Service

All Rights Reserved © 2023 by Roderick L. Evans

No part of this book may be reproduced or transmitted in any form or by any means, graphic, electronic, or mechanical, including photocopying, recording, taping or by any information storage or retrieval system, without the permission in writing from the publisher. Front & Back Cover Designs by Abundant Truth Publishing

Front & Back Cover Designs by Abundant Truth International Publishing
Image by Arnie Bragg from Pixabay

Abundant Truth Publishing
an imprint of Abundant Truth International Ministries
For information address:
Abundant Truth International
P.O. Box 126
Camden, NC 27921

ISBN 13: 978-1-60141-529-5

Printed in the United States of America

Unless otherwise indicated, all of the scripture quotations are taken from the *Authorized King James Version* of the Bible. Scripture quotations marked with NIV are taken from the *New International Version* of the Bible. Scripture quotations marked with NASV are taken from the *New American Standard Version* of the Bible. Scripture quotations marked with Amplified are taken from the *Amplified Bible*.

Contents

Introduction

Chapter 1 – The Motive of Love   1

Example of Jesus   *7*
Example of the Apostles   *14*

Chapter 2 – The Motive of Obedience   25

Example of Jesus   *28*
Example of the Apostles   *39*
Excuses: The Enemy of Obedience   *45*

Chapter 3 – Motives to Avoid   57

Price   *62*

Contents (cont.)

People   *71*
Personal Gain   *77*

Bibliography   **85**

Introduction

God anoints and endows individuals with gifts and talents to serve in the Church. However, some have missed the very purpose of gifts and ministries in the Church. In the Abundant Truth Leadership Series, we will endeavor to present a proper foundation for believers to minister upon.

In this publication

What is motive? How do we define motivation? Motive/motivation is defined as something (as a need or desire) that causes a person to act. So then, what causes us to do what we do in the Kingdom?

What are the forces driving you to want to minister? Why do you want God to use you? Why do you allow God to use you? Self-inventory has to be taken on a regular basis.

Examine yourselves, whether ye be in the faith; prove your own selves. (2 Corinthians 13:5a)

For if we would judge ourselves, we should not be judged. (2 Corinthians 11:31)

In the second book of this series, we learn that it is only through self-examination that our motives in ministry and service remain pure. As leaders and servants in the Church and kingdom of God, we can lose focus on God's plan and purpose for ministry. In this brief study, we will examine the proper motives for ministry and those to avoid.

-Chapter 1-

The Motive of Love

MOTIVES IN MINISTRY

Defining the Proper Motives for Ministry and Service

MOTIVES IN MINISTRY

Defining the Proper Motives for Ministry and Service

To begin our discussion, we want to look at the foundational motive for ministry that leaders and servants bmust possess – LOVE. If we are to minister effectively, love is the primary component.

If you do not love Him and His people, your motivation for ministry is tainted by other impulses. Love has many attributes. It is patient, kind, not easily provoked, it is not puffed up, and the like.

We see many in the Church

claiming to minister in the Spirit, but there is no love felt in their ministry. God is love. Everything that He does for us is through love. Ministry without love is valueless in the eyes of the Lord.

> *Though I speak with the tongues of men and of angels, and have not charity (love), I am become as sounding brass, or a tinkling cymbal. And though I have the gift of prophecy, and understand all mysteries, and all knowledge; and*

though I have all faith, so that I could remove mountains, and have not charity, I am nothing. And though I bestow all my goods to feed the poor, and though I give my body to be burned, and have not charity, it profiteth me nothing. (I Corinthians 13:1-3 parenthesis mine)

Leaders and servants must pray that the love of God rules in their hearts. Love serves as an umpire in ministry.

Without love, ministry becomes a burden, rather than a commitment to serve. As we look at how love motivated Jesus and the apostles, let us remember the characteristics of love.

Charity suffereth long, and is kind; charity envieth not; charity vaunteth not itself, is not puffed up, Doth not behave itself unseemly, seeketh Beareth all things, believeth all things, hopeth all things, endureth all things. Charity never faileth... (I Corinthians 13:4-8a)

Ministry without love breeds chaos, competition, and resentment. Love brings order and balance to the revelation and power of God being displayed among His people.***

Example of Jesus

From the gospels, we understand that Jesus was an obedient Son to the Father which characterized His earthly ministry. Presently, we shall see how love motivated Jesus in ministry. There are numerous accounts of Jesus being moved by love and compassion. The result was ministry. Consider the following passages of scripture:

> And Jesus, when he came out, saw much people, and was moved with compassion toward them, because they were as sheep not having a shepherd: and he began to teach them many things. (Mark 6:34)

His teaching ministry was fueled by love. Many preach, teach, sing, and serve today for popularity and acclaim.

This has produced knowledgeable people who have not received true ministry. Their faith oftentimes rests in eloquent speech, performances, and entertainment rather than in the Lord.

And Jesus went forth, and saw a great multitude, and was moved with compassion toward them, and he] healed their sick. (Matthew 14:14)

Jesus showed the same level of compassion in crowds and in smaller settings. He did not minister to impress the multitudes. Make sure this is not a pitfall for you as a leader and/or servant. Never have the crowd-pleasing motive.

Be motivated to bless one individual as you would to minister and serve one thousand individuals.

And Jesus, moved with compassion, put forth his hand, and touched him, and saith unto him, I will; be thou clean. And as soon as he had spoken, immediately the leprosy departed from him, and he was cleansed. (Mark 1:41-42)

In each of the above verses, we find that love preceded ministry. If you want effective, pure service, the motivation of love will guarantee it. Before he healed the sick in the multitude, healed the leper, and taught the crowds, Jesus was moved by love and compassion. Though he faced rejection, He continued to minister.

He came unto his own, and his own received him not. (John 1:11)

He is despised and rejected of men; a man of sorrows, and acquainted with grief: and we hid as it were our faces from him; he was despised, and we esteemed him not. (Isaiah 53:3)

Jesus' ministry consistently faced rejection. Can we continue to minister and serve being motivated by love when we are rejected? If Jesus could overcome the negative responses of men and have a fruitful and powerful ministry, we can also. His example is our standard for ministry and service.

We cannot minister effectively if we do not love those to whom we minister. Your ministry and service is received without hindrance when your motivation is love. It is a requirement for service in the Church. Many individuals minister and serve, but do not love the people of the Lord.

This leads to critical statements and harsh gestures while ministering in the name of the Lord. Without love, your ministry will not last or you will slip into error.

Love causes you to be more attentive to the need of the individual and the voice of the Lord. Love is a safeguard against deception. Without love, the wrong motives will subdue you. ***

Example of the Apostles

In their writings, the apostles demonstrated that they were motivated by love. We will look at some of the writings of Paul and John to show that the greatest of the apostles ministered through love. Their love for the saints mirrored the love of the Father.

Paul

While writing to the Corinthians, Paul expressed his love and concern for them in both of his letters. He did this in spite of their disobedience to the Word and their challenge of his authority and office.

Behold, the third time I am ready to come to you; and I will not be burdensome to you: for I seek not yours, but you: for the children ought not to lay up for the parents, but the parents for the children. And I will very gladly spend and be spent for you; though the more abundantly I love you, the less I be loved. (II Corinthians 12:14- 15)

He loved the Church with a fatherly love. He compared His love to that of a parent and child. He told them that he would gladly give all that he had for them, though they rejected him. This demonstrates that his motivation was love. Though they challenged, criticized, and rejected him, he did not waiver from ministry.

Regardless of your ministry and service, you cannot allow the negative responses of men to stop you. If you are motivated by love, it will cover the multitude of faults in others. It will keep you focused on your objective to render serve while representing the nature of God.

Remember, God is kind to the

thankful and evil. We have to remain willing to minister in love to others even when they act unappreciative.

John

In his writings to the saints, John used expressions of love to show that he ministered to the saints through the motivation of love.

> *My little children, these things write unto you, that ye sin not. And if any man sin, we have an advocate with the Father, Jesus Christ the righteous. (I John 2:1)*

I have no greater joy than to hear that my children walk in truth. (3 John verse 4)

Paul, John expressed a genuine fatherly concern for the Church. Though he experienced the revelation of God and walked with Christ, his motivation for ministry remained rooted in love.

He and Paul show us that regardless of our status in the Kingdom, love can remain the primary motivation. This proves to be an important truth.

Some, after operating in effective ministry and serve begin to feel that they are above others and should be served rather than serve. If Paul and John continued to love, it is our responsibility (as those given the privilege to serve) to love the Church as we minister within its parameters.

MOTIVES IN MINISTRY
Defining the Proper Motives for Ministry and Service

Notes:

MOTIVES IN MINISTRY
Defining the Proper Motives for Ministry and Service

_____

_____

_____

_____

_____

_____

_____

_____

_____

-Chapter 2-

The Motive of Obedience

MOTIVES IN MINISTRY

Defining the Proper Motives for Ministry and Service

MOTIVES IN MINISTRY
Defining the Proper Motives for Ministry and Service

Aside from love, the only other motive that one should have for ministry is obedience. Some may say, shouldn't there be other motives. There are other good motives, but there is a potential for those to become warped.

Outside of love for God and His people, and obedience to God's plan and purpose, one sets his/herself up for improper motives.

Though it is good to want to be known for your good works and leave a legacy for others to follow, these could turn overtly selfish and taint your ministry and service.

Therefore, obedience to God has to be the other foundational element of your motivation in ministry and service. Jesus and the apostles demonstrated that they were motivated by obedience to God. If we follow their examples, we too can incorporate obedience to God as motivation for ministry.***

Example of Jesus

Jesus repeatedly reminded His followers that He came to do the will (obey) His Father. Christ was sent, to give His life, by the Father. The writer of Hebrews quotes a Messianic prophecy to attest to this fact.

Then said I, Lo, I come (in the volume of the book it is written of me,) to do thy will, O God. (Hebrews 10:7)

Though He was the Son of God, He did not do what He wanted to do. He did not work miracles, heal the sick, or even preach without it being in obedience to the Father. We, too, are to minister by the will of God. God allows us to serve to accomplish His will. Our gifts and ministries are to be administered at His discretion and not our desire.

Maintaining the motive of obedience will guard against wrong motives for displaying and demonstrating our gifts. This is needed because many influences, internal and external, are present. If not recognized, our motives in ministry will become negatively influenced.

MOTIVES IN MINISTRY
Defining the Proper Motives for Ministry and Service

I speak that which I have seen with my Father: and ye do that which ye have seen with your father. (John 8:38)

He was the Lord of all and yet, He humbled Himself before God. Jesus did not operate out of vain motives or for selfish gain. We have to follow the Lord's morality and motivation in ministry.

Who, being in the form of God, thought it not robbery to be equal with God: but made himself of no reputation, and took upon him the form of a servant, and was made in the likeness of men: And being found in fashion as a man, he humbled himself, and became obedient unto death, even the death of the cross. (Philippians 2:6-8)

Jesus had the attitude of a servant. Today, we find many leaders and servants who do not have this mindset. They want to be served and to build their own empires. This is why ministry and service can become ritualistic and ineffective. Even with the temptation in the wilderness to demonstrate His power, He maintained His integrity.

And when the tempter came to him, he said, If thou be the Son of God, command that these stones be made bread. But he answered and said, It is written, Man shall not live by bread alone, but by every word that proceedeth out of the mouth of God. (Matthew 4:3-4)

MOTIVES IN MINISTRY
Defining the Proper Motives for Ministry and Service

Many Christians fall because they want to prove to others that they have gifts. We sometimes forget ministries are given to serve others. Ministry is not for self-promotion.

Christ came to glorify God in His ministry. Everything that He did, He consistently claimed that He was motivated by obedience to the Father.

For I came down from heaven, not to do mine own will, but the will of him that sent me. (John 6:38)

I can of mine own self do nothing: as I hear, I judge: and my judgment is just; because I seek not mine own will, but the will of the Father which hath sent me. (John 5:30)

If we do not adopt this attitude, we will fall into the snare of the devil. Temptations are all around us. The gifts and ministries of God draw attention and favor from men.

We have to desire usability and not visibility. However, our motives must remain pure. Jesus never deviated from doing all things through obedience.

Many anointed, gifted, and talented individuals have erred because they forgot that it was not about them or their ministries, but about God. Jesus came from glory, and He still stated that He could not do anything of Himself. Yet, we find many believers today boasting and trusting in their abilities and gifts as if they earned or deserved them.

And these things, brethren, I have in a figure transferred to myself and to Apollos for your sakes; that ye might learn in us not to think of men above that which is written, that no one of you be puffed up for one against another. For who maketh thee to differ from another? And what hast thou that thou didst not receive? Now if thou didst receive it, why dost thou glory, as if thou hadst not received it? (I Corinthians 4:6-7)

Paul told his readers that they are not to lift up men or be puffed up against one another because of varying gifts. We are to resist this at all costs. We have to remember that God gave us every gift that we have.

He knows how we are to use them. We have to seek His will as did Christ. Obedience has to be a governing motivation in our ministry and service as it was with Christ. ***

Example of the Apostles

The apostles were also motivated by obedience to God. After the resurrection and the outpouring of the Spirit, the apostles began to preach in His name. We find that even under the threat of imprisonment and death, they proclaimed that they would be obedient to God.

And when they had brought them, they set them before the council: and the high priest asked them, Saying, Did not we straightly command you that ye should not teach in this name? And, behold, ye have filled Jerusalem with your doctrine, and intend to bring this man's blood upon us. Then Peter and the other apostles answered and said, We ought to obey God rather than men. (Acts 5:27-29)

They were not concerned about making names for themselves as many are today. They wanted to make known the reality of God and of Christ. We have to be willing to minister and serve even in light of opposition. Obedience helps the leader and servant to do this.

We discover also that Paul had a profound sense of obedience in ministry. He understood that he ministered with great power and authority only by obedience. Leaders and servants must remember that their service in the Church is effective when rendered in obedience.

We are fools for Christ's sake, but ye are wise in Christ; we are weak, but ye are strong; ye are honourable, but we are despised. Even unto this present hour we both hunger, and thirst, and are naked, and are buffeted, and have no certain dwelling place; And labour, working with our own hands: being reviled, we bless; being persecuted, we suffer it: Being defamed, we entreat: we are made as the filth of the world, and are the off scouring of all things unto this day. (I Corinthians 4:10 - 13)

Paul began this address by calling himself a fool because of Christ. He was implying that all of the trials and tests that he experienced were due to his obedience to the call of God. His motivation to be obedient to the call of God encouraged him to endure all things.

Paul knew that God had called him from the womb and that He was alive only to serve Him.

But when it pleased God, who separated me from my mother's womb, and called me by his grace, to reveal his Son in me, that I might preach him among the heathen. (Galatians 1:15-16a)

Like Paul, we must accept the difficulties that come as a result of ministry and service, knowing that God has purpose for what He has called us to do. We must use our gifts and ministries through obedience.

If the motivation of obedience is lost, wrong motives will surface, or we will

want to quit when troubles arise.

Remember, we minister and serve because God commands it, not because we desire it or it is always received favorably.***

Excuses, The Enemy of Obedience

We could not conclude our brief examination on obeying God if we do not discuss the excuses we use for disobedience.

Though there are many, here are three commonly used excuses for not obeying God:

MOTIVES IN MINISTRY
Defining the Proper Motives for Ministry and Service

1) People will not receive me

2) I do not know what to do when I hear from God.

3) I do not want to go into error.

PEOPLE WILL NOT RECEIVE ME

Success in ministry is never to be judged by the response of the people. Success in ministry is based upon your obedience to God.

There are numerous examples of God's servants being successful in ministry without the warm reception of their listeners.

And thou, son of man, be not afraid of them, neither be afraid of their words, though briers and thorns be with thee, and thou dost dwell among scorpions: be not afraid of their words, nor be dismayed at their looks, though they be a rebellious house. (Ezekiel 2:6)

He told Ezekiel from the beginning that the people were not going to hear him, but he was to prophesy anyway. How about that job description?

There are times when people will reject the ministry of God in you. You have to remember not to confuse the rejection of ministry with personal rejection.

We are under a New Covenant in which the Spirit is in all who have truly believed. There will be more that receive you than those who do not. This excuse is born out of a fear of rejection. It must be overcome because God does not receive our excuses for disobedience.

Defining the Proper Motives for Ministry and Service

I DO NOT KNOW WHAT TO DO WHEN I HEAR FROM GOD & I DO NOT WANT TO GO INTO ERROR

These two excuses are born out of fear combined with slothfulness. This same excuse was used by the steward who buried his talent. He blamed the master for being too hard and did not want to make mistakes with the money.

When His master returned, he called him wicked and lazy. He would not have given him the talent if he did not know what to do with it.

Then he which had received the one talent came and said, Lord, I knew thee that thou art an hard man, reaping where thou hast not sown, and gathering where thou hast not strewed: And I was afraid, and went and hid thy talent in the earth: lo, there thou hast that is thine. His lord answered and said unto him, Thou wicked and slothful servant, thou knewest that I reap where I sowed not, and gather where I have not strewed:

Thou oughtest therefore to have put my money to the exchangers, and then at my coming I should have received mine own with usury. (Matthew 25:24-27)

God is likened unto the master in this parable. God will not give us gifts and not give us understanding of how they work or how to use them. Oftentimes, we claim ignorance so that no action has to take place on our part.

Believers lie to themselves all the time about whether or not they are called. It is easier to say I do know if it is God than risk stepping out and being rejected or wrong. Avoid excuses at all costs. They are the enemies of obedient servants.

MOTIVES IN MINISTRY
Defining the Proper Motives for Ministry and Service

Notes:

MOTIVES IN MINISTRY
Defining the Proper Motives for Ministry and Service

-Chapter 3-

The Motives to Avoid

MOTIVES IN MINISTRY
Defining the Proper Motives for Ministry and Service

MOTIVES IN MINISTRY
Defining the Proper Motives for Ministry and Service

It is important not only to know the motives to have, but also those to avoid. If leaders and servants are motivated by obedience and love, they will have fruitful ministries.

Without these, leaders and servants will fall into condemnation and a snare of the devil. God may have to use discipline for improper motives in His service.

The keys to avoiding wrong motives are *Prayer*, *Honesty*, and *Humility*. Prayer keeps you in touch with the Spirit of God who can reveal the hidden motives of the heart.

In addition, it brings clarity to the needs of others that our ministry to them is precise and timely. Honesty helps you to acknowledge your faults. Humility helps you to receive correction and instruction from others.

> *Reprove not a scorner, lest he hate thee: rebuke a wise man, and he will love thee. Give instruction to a wise man, and he will be yet wiser: teach a just man, and he will*

increase in learning. (Proverbs 9:8-9)

If you receive instruction and correction, you will become a wise leader or servant. Wisdom guards against improper motives.

Though numerous motives exist in ministry, we will examine the wrong motives of price, people, and personal gain. These wrong motives are seen readily in many believers. We will explore scriptural examples of men operating in wrong motives, and the consequences. ***

Price

Men have been seduced for centuries by money. Many ministers today are using scriptures to justify their greed, lust, and love of money. The scriptures say that the love of money is the root of all evil.

For the love of money is the root of all evil: which while some coveted after, they have erred from the faith, and pierced themselves through with many sorrows. (I Timothy 6:10)

Never use your gift or ministry for financial gain. Don't serve for the dollar. If you are called to preach, it has to be done without price; that is, without money determining the bounds of when and where you will preach the gospel.

We receive gifts freely from God and God expects us to minister to one another freely. He offered salvation to us without price. Isaiah attested to this when he prophesied,

Ho, every one that thirsteth, come ye to the waters, and he that hath no money; come ye, buy, and eat; yea, come, buy wine and milk without money and without price. (Isaiah 55:1)

Through the prophet, God was offering salvation to Israel without price. Christ did the same for us. Even individuals who are not called to preach have learned how to use their gifts for gain. Many do not serve in ministry for the love of God, but for hope of financial support.

The scriptures give many examples of men who erred from the faith because of money. One well known account is found in II Kings. Elisha turned down reward from Naaman who was healed of leprosy.

And he returned to the man of God, he and all his company, and came, and stood before him: and he said, Behold, now I know that there is no God in all the earth, but in Israel: now therefore, I

> *pray thee, take a blessing of thy servant. But he said, As the Lord liveth, before whom I stand, I will receive none. And he urged him to take it; but he refused. (II Kings 5:15-16)*

However, his servant, Gehazi, lied to Naaman in order to receive what Elisha had refused. He used ministry for gain.

> *But Gehazi, the servant of Elisha the man of God, said, Behold, my master hath spared Naaman this*

Syrian, in not receiving at his hands that which he brought: but, as the Lord liveth, I will run after him, and take somewhat of him. So Gehazi followed after Naaman. And when Naaman saw him running after him, he lighted down from the chariot to meet him, and said, Is all well? And he said, All is well. My master hath sent me, saying, Behold, even now there be come to me from mount Ephraim two young men of the sons of the prophets: give them, I pray thee, a talent of silver, and two changes of garments. (II Kings 5:20-22)

Later, we find that the Lord judged him for his greediness. Naaman's leprosy came upon him.

And he said unto him, Went not mine heart with thee, when the man turned again from his chariot to meet thee? Is it a time to receive money, and to receive garments, and oliveyards, and vineyards, and sheep, and oxen, and menservants, and maidservants? The leprosy therefore of Naaman shall cleave unto thee, and unto thy seed for ever. And he went out from his presence a leper as white as snow. (II Kings 5:26-27)

Wrong motives will always lead to other sins. Gehazi's wrong motive caused him to lie. When your motives are wrong, you will do things to cover them up. Do not allow your service to corrupt you and your ministry to mess up your walk with Christ.

Wrong motives will cause ministry and service that was meant to bless you and others to become a destructive force in the life of the Church. This is why it is vital to be honest with oneself.

It was common in Israel that the servant of the prophet would be in line to become a prophet. However, his future ministry was cancelled and the family line cursed. Wrong motives will be death to any genuine ministry. In the Church, we have learned to sow financial seeds to people who have blessed us.

If you are used frequently in the gifts, it is common for people to offer you many things in appreciation. Be on guard that you never prophesy or encourage anyone for money. ***

People

The praise of men can be intoxicating to the ego. It is easy to be seduced by the admiration and adulation of men. However, performing to receive the praises of men is detrimental to any ministry.

Recognizing this motive in ministry can be difficult at times. It is common for people to speak of how we have blessed them, especially if our ministry to them came at a crucial moment.

Individuals who have ministries that are on display (singing, preaching, prophesying, playing instruments, etc.) are vulnerable in particular. The praises and thanks of people can be addictive. Saul, Israel's first king, ruined

MOTIVES IN MINISTRY
Defining the Proper Motives for Ministry and Service

his ministry as king because of people.

And Samuel said, What hast thou done? And Saul said, Because I saw that the people were scattered from me, and that thou camest not within the days appointed, and that the Philistines gathered themselves together at Michmash. Therefore, said I, The Philistines will come down now upon me to Gilgal, and I have not made supplication unto the Lord: I forced myself therefore, and offered a burnt offering. (I Samuel 13:11- 12)

Saul was supposed to wait for Samuel to make the sacrifice to God. He allowed the pressure of people to force him into doing something only reserved for the priests.

He was new to the throne and wanted to show the people (under Philistines threat) that he could lead. He feared the people would not want him as king because some had already left him. The result was that the kingdom was taken away from him and his seed.

But now thy kingdom shall not continue: the Lord hath sought him a man after his own heart, and the Lord hath commanded him to be captain over his people, because thou hast not kept that which the Lord commanded thee. (I Samuel 13:14)

We learn some important lessons from from Saul. First, when People are your motive for ministry, you will do things that you are not gifted or called to do. You will minister beyond your measure of anointing. Second, God will not allow it. He cut his kingship short. You will pay the same price if you make people your motivation for ministry. Paul said,

> *For do I now persuade men, or God? Or do I seek to please men? For if I yet pleased men, I should not be the servant of Christ. (Galatians 1:10)*

He told them it would be impossible impossible to serve God and man. We have to make a decision as to whom we will serve in ministry. If you cannot handle man's rejection and ridicule, you are not ready for ministry.***

Personal Gain

This final wrong motive is hard to detect. Personal gain is usually interpreted as money. However, personal gain is subjective to the individual. Some people use ministry as therapy for their own physical and emotional needs.

There are individuals who have low

self-esteem, never had many friends, never received love, and the like. Ministry to them becomes a form of establishing self-worth and identity for them.

> *For they bind heavy burdens and grievous to be borne, and lay them on men's shoulders; but they themselves will not move them with one of their fingers. But all their works they do for to be seen of men: they make broad their phylacteries, and enlarge the*

borders of their garments, And love the uppermost rooms at feasts, and the chief seats in the synagogues, And greetings in the markets, and to be called of men, Rabbi, Rabbi. (Matthew 23:4-7)

The Pharisees are examples of this type of motive in ministry. They loved to make themselves seem spiritual and important so that men would look up to them and respect them. They used religious service to establish their identities and self-worth.

MOTIVES IN MINISTRY
Defining the Proper Motives for Ministry and Service

You have to be honest and recognize if you are vulnerable in this area. It can prove to be deadly to your ministry.

Self-examination is the key to maintaining pure motives in ministry. If you learn to judge your own motives through the Word of God and by the Spirit, the flesh will not overtake you in this area.

Remember the foundation for your motives for ministry has to be love and obedience. In doing so, your leadership and service in the Church will abound to the spiritual growth and enhancement of many.

MOTIVES IN MINISTRY
Defining the Proper Motives for Ministry and Service

MOTIVES IN MINISTRY
Defining the Proper Motives for Ministry and Service

Notes:

_____

_____

_____

_____

_____

_____

_____

MOTIVES IN MINISTRY
Defining the Proper Motives for Ministry and Service

Bibliography

Smith, William. Smith's Bible Dictionary. Holman Bible Publishers. Nashville, Tennessee. c1994

The Bible Library. The Bible Library CD Rom Disc. Ellis Enterprises Incorporated, (c)1988 – 2000. 4205 McAuley Blvd., Suite 385, Oklahoma City, OK 73120. All Rights Reserved.

Lockman Foundation. Comparative Study Bible. Zondervan Publishing House. Grand Rapids, MI, c1984

MOTIVES IN MINISTRY
Defining the Proper Motives for Ministry and Service

Notes:

_____

_____

_____

_____

_____

_____

_____

_____

MOTIVES IN MINISTRY

Defining the Proper Motives for Ministry and Service

Notes:

MOTIVES IN MINISTRY

Defining the Proper Motives for Ministry and Service

www.ingramcontent.com/pod-product-compliance
Lightning Source LLC
Chambersburg PA
CBHW050343010526
44119CB00049B/673